CBT Thrive

James Alexander Hamilton

Mile's Ahead publishing

Unity, celebration, and the positive impact of embracing diverse cultures, all of which contribute to the holistic approach of CBT

Table of Contents

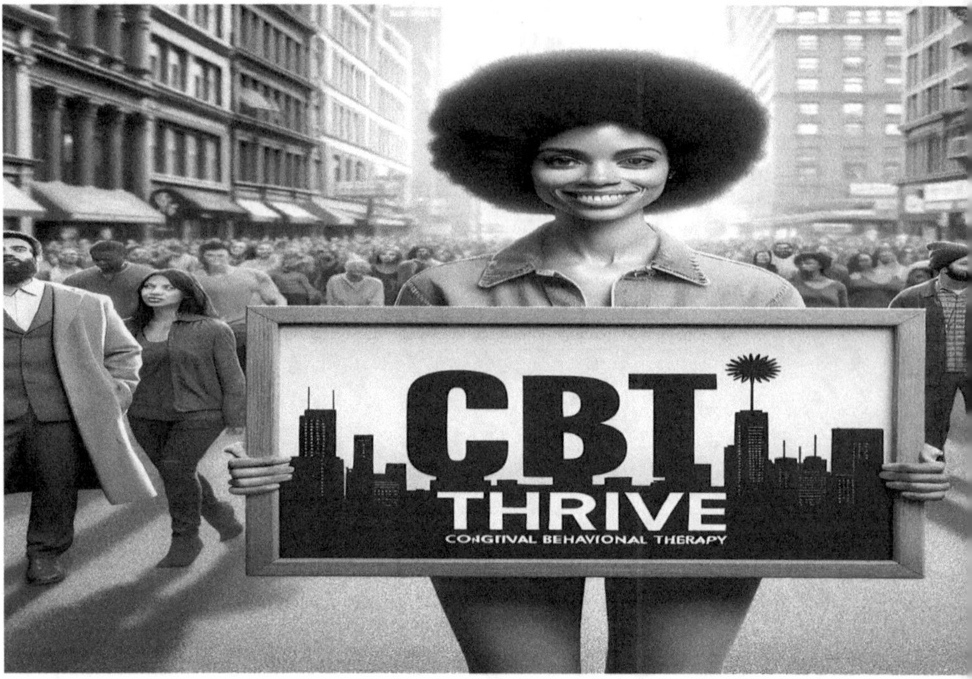

CBT
THRIVE
COGNITIVE BEHAVIORAL THERAPY

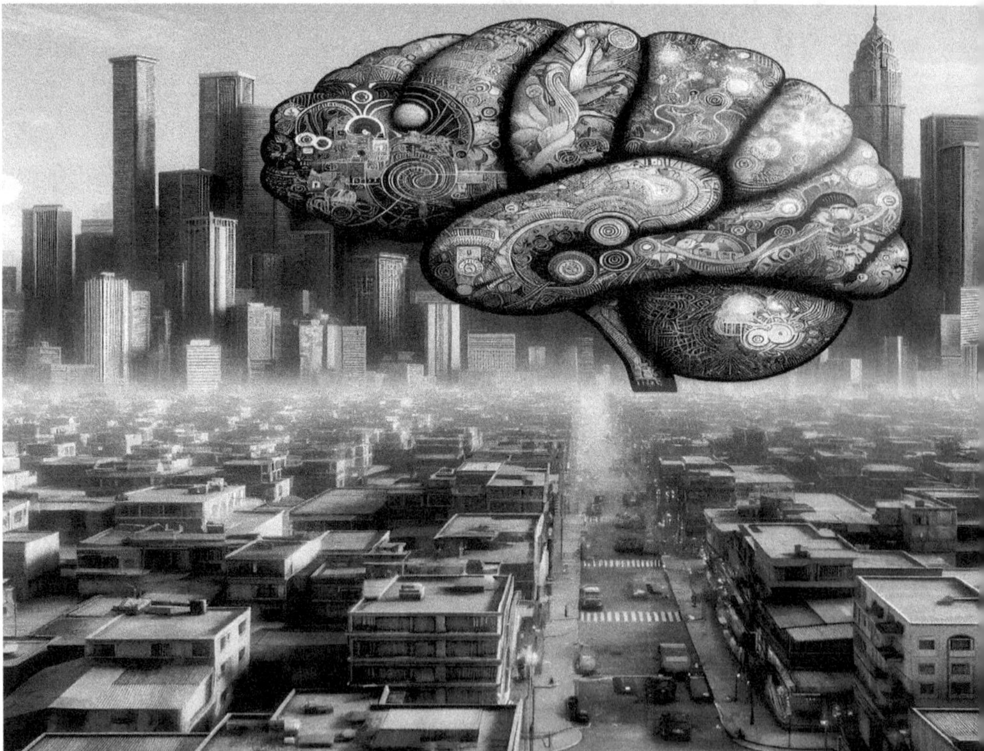

Chapter 1

In the heart of Chicago Heights, Illinois, where the walls echoed stories of families torn apart and children lost, the soil of my mind began its journey. It was a place where poverty wasn't just a state of financial deprivation, but a profound mental challenge. The neighborhood was a patchwork of life experiences, each plot bearing the marks of struggles and dreams that had taken root in its confines.

Understanding our Mind's Landscape:

The human mind is a vast terrain, with valleys of doubt and peaks of confidence. Growing up, my landscape was dotted with the towering figures of my grandmother, Mary Moses, and Pastor Robert Moses. They were the gardeners of my young psyche, planting seeds of faith and wisdom.

Through the pages of the Bible, I was introduced to the ancient form of CBT. Scriptures, which spoke to each reader in a unique voice, provided solace and guidance, much like the therapeutic techniques of Cognitive Behavioral Therapy. They taught me to introspect, to challenge my beliefs, and to seek the truth within. The words flowed like a river, nurturing the seeds of self-worth and purpose, teaching me that even in the darkest moments, one could find a glimmer of hope.

However, as time wore on, the challenges grew. Schools, which were once places of learning, turned into battlegrounds. The corridors echoed with the sounds of fights and confrontations, while the classrooms bore witness to teachers struggling to maintain order. The pressures of the digital age, combined with the weight of societal expectations, began to erode the mental landscapes of many young minds. The absence of proper guidance and support turned these fertile grounds into barren wastelands.

The Importance of a Healthy Start:

My early years were shaped by the loving care of my family and the teachings of the church. These influences acted as the fertilizers that enriched my mental soil, ensuring that the seeds of positivity and resilience took root firmly. But not everyone was as fortunate. The tragic events that unfolded in front of my home on that fateful day were a stark reminder of the importance of nurturing our mental gardens from a young age.

The sounds of celebration following my daughter's volleyball victory were abruptly replaced by the heart-wrenching cries of a community in mourning. A young life, full of potential, was cut short in a senseless act of violence. The perpetrators, barely out of childhood themselves, were products of a system that had failed them. Their minds, which should have been gardens of creativity and ambition, had turned into breeding grounds for anger and resentment.

In the face of such tragedies, one cannot help but wonder: What if these young souls had been given the right tools and guidance from the beginning? What if their mental landscapes had been cared for and nurtured, ensuring that the seeds of negativity were weeded out before they took root? The importance of a healthy start cannot be overstated. Our minds are like gardens, and the seeds we plant in our formative years determine the kind of harvest we reap in adulthood.

As I reflect on my own journey, I realize that the foundation of our mental well-being lies in understanding our mind's landscape and recognizing the importance of a healthy start. It's time we prioritize the mental gardens of our youth, ensuring that they are equipped with the tools and knowledge to thrive in a world that is constantly evolving.

Nurturing the Seedlings:

Growing up in Chicago Heights, I was surrounded by a multitude of stories, each more poignant than the last. Yet, amidst the chaos and hardships, there were beacons of hope, guiding lights that showed the way. My grandmother, Mary Moses, was one such beacon. Her dedication as a missionary for the Church of God in Christ was a testament to her unwavering faith and commitment to bettering the lives of those around her.

Her teachings, rooted deeply in the scriptures, became my first introduction to the transformative power of words. The Bible, with its tales of trials, tribulations, and triumphs, served as a metaphorical mirror, reflecting the challenges of our own lives. Through its verses, I learned the art of self-reflection, of questioning, and of seeking understanding. This, in essence, was my first brush with the principles of Cognitive Behavioral Therapy (CBT).

The Power of Perspective:

The world is a complex tapestry of experiences and emotions. Every individual, every child, views it through a unique lens shaped by their upbringing, culture, and personal experiences. The mind's landscape, much like a physical garden, requires attention, care, and, most importantly, the right perspective.

In my formative years, watching families grapple with challenges, witnessing the strength and resilience of my community, I came to understand the significance of perspective. It's not the challenges that define us, but how we perceive and respond to them. CBT emphasizes this very idea – the power to reshape our reactions by altering our perspectives.

Tending to Our Mental Garden:

As the years went by, I began to see the ripple effects of early influences on young minds. The school corridors, which once echoed with laughter and learning, became arenas of conflict. The digital age, with its barrage of information and influences, began to muddy the clear waters of young minds. Social media platforms became the new battlegrounds, where self-worth was measured in likes, shares, and comments.

Yet, amidst this digital chaos, the principles of CBT shone like a guiding star. By recognizing and challenging

CBT stands for Cognitive Behavioral Therapy. It's a type of psychotherapy or talk therapy that focuses on helping individuals identify and change negative thought patterns and behaviors. CBT is commonly used to treat various mental health conditions, such as depression, anxiety disorders, phobias, and post-traumatic stress disorder. It aims to help people develop healthier ways of thinking and coping with their emotions, ultimately leading to improved mental well-being. I genuinely think that CBT therapy could make a real difference in saving many young lives, but it's gotta be presented to them in a way that hits home. So many folks out there ain't aware that it's all about flipping the script on how they think and how they talk to themselves. That shift in mindset can be a game-changer, transforming their whole perspective on life. We need to do everything in our power to rescue our youth. Please, let's work together to make this happen.

negative thought patterns, by focusing on the present and cultivating mindfulness, one could navigate the treacherous waters of adolescence and beyond.

Planting Seeds of Hope:

The tragic incident in front of my home, where a young life was snuffed out in its prime, was a grim reminder of the urgency to act. Our youth, teetering on the edge, need guidance, support, and tools to help them make sense of the world around them. CBT offers a beacon of hope in this regard.

By teaching young minds to recognize, challenge, and replace negative thought patterns with positive ones, CBT lays the groundwork for a mentally healthy adulthood. It provides the tools to cultivate resilience, empathy, and emotional intelligence – skills that are crucial in today's fast-paced world.

The soil of our minds, like that of a garden, is fertile ground, waiting to be sowed with seeds of positivity, hope, and resilience. By understanding our mind's landscape, recognizing the importance of early influences, and equipping our youth with the tools of CBT, we can ensure that the gardens of their minds bloom with flowers of happiness, contentment, and success. The journey might be long and fraught with challenges, but with the right care and nurturing, every mind can thrive.

Preparing the Soil

Chapter 2

The symphony of life isn't just about the harmonious notes; it's also about the dissonances, the pauses, and the crescendos. Among the bouquets of blossoming flowers, weeds persistently sprout, seeking their space under the sun. Just like in our societies, these weeds represent challenges, traumas, and other negative influences that, if ignored, might overshadow the vibrant blooms. Our narrative today revolves around such a weed, which, with the right care, has the potential to bloom.

Nigel's Odyssey: A Tale from Chicago Heights

Chicago Heights, Illinois, once a flourishing industrial hub, had seen better days. The echoes of prosperity

were now replaced by the haunting silence of desolation. Amidst this backdrop, our protagonist, Nigel, a young African-American, navigated his tumultuous teenage years.

Growing up in this environment, Nigel was no stranger to challenges. The cacophony of gang violence, the grim specter of poverty, and the lure of the streets cast long shadows over his early life. Yet, beneath the tough exterior was a young man yearning for acceptance, guidance, and, most importantly, a purpose.

A Star Dimmed

Once the pride of his school's football team, Nigel's agility on the field earned him accolades and admiration. But as senior year approached, the trajectory of his life took a sharp turn. A single event, a strong-arm robbery charge, cast a pall over his promising future. Overnight, the star athlete became the 'problem child.' The corridors that once echoed with cheers now whispered tales of his fall from grace.

Mrs. Davis: A Beacon in the Storm

In the vast sea of judgment, one voice stood out, offering solace and understanding—Mrs. Davis. A teacher with a background in Cognitive Behavioral Therapy (CBT), she saw potential where others saw problems. To her, Nigel wasn't just another statistic; he was a young mind, scarred by his environment but not defined by it.

Their first significant interaction happened on a day Nigel would never forget. The weight of the world pressing down on him, a seemingly insignificant altercation with a teacher, Mr. Ameri, became the tipping point. Words were exchanged, tempers flared, and in a moment of unbridled anger, desks were overturned. The entire school was abuzz with whispers and pointed fingers.

However, Mrs. Davis saw beyond the outburst. She recognized it for what it was—a desperate cry for help.

The Therapy of Affirmation

Introducing Nigel to the principles of CBT, Mrs. Davis emphasized the power of positive affirmations. She believed that by challenging and replacing his internal negative narratives, Nigel could reshape his reality. Every day, she'd remind him, "You are not defined by your past, but by the choices you make today. You have the potential to change, to grow, to shine."

She introduced him to journaling, encouraging him to confront his fears and traumas on paper. These sessions became therapeutic, a safe haven for Nigel to introspect, reflect, and envision a brighter future.

Nana: The Pillar of Strength

Another beacon in Nigel's life was his grandmother, affectionately known as Nana. A devout woman with deep roots in missionary work, she embodied faith and resilience. Every night, she'd share stories from the Bible, emphasizing themes of redemption, hope, and transformation. To her, these ancient tales weren't mere history but lessons on the indomitable human spirit.

A Wake-Up Call

One brisk evening, as winter's chill began to settle in, Nigel's usual walk home took a detour into the unexpected. The park, typically a haven for kids playing after school, was transformed into a somber tableau. A makeshift memorial of candles, flowers, and notes stood

at the basketball court's edge. A young boy, just a year older than Nigel, had been caught in the crossfire of a drive-by shooting while playing a pick-up game.

The eeriness of the silent park, juxtaposed against the vibrant memories of laughter and games, struck a deep chord within Nigel. The impermanence of life and the unpredictability of fate became startlingly clear.

Mrs. Davis, sensing the shift in Nigel's demeanor the following day at school, took it upon herself to guide him through this traumatic experience. She emphasized the power of resilience and the importance of finding constructive ways to channel grief and anger. Drawing upon her knowledge of Cognitive Behavioral Therapy, she equipped Nigel with tools to process his feelings and transform them into a force for positive change in his community.

The Road to Redemption

With time, therapy, and relentless support from Mrs. Davis and Nana, Nigel began to transform. The anger that once consumed him gave way to determination. The de-

spair was replaced by dreams. The young man who once saw himself as a product of his environment now aspired to change it.

A Society's Role

Nigel's story isn't an isolated one. Countless youths, especially in underserved communities, grapple with similar challenges. The external weeds of societal judgment, peer pressure, and economic hardships often give rise to internal weeds of self-doubt, anxiety, and depression.

However, with the right interventions, support systems, and therapeutic approaches, these weeds can be uprooted. The onus is on society to recognize and nurture the potential in every individual, ensuring that they don't get lost in the intricate pattern of life.

The Legacy of CBT: Dr. Aaron Beck's Vision

It was Dr. Aaron Beck who illuminated the path for countless individuals like Nigel. Recognizing the profound impact of internal narratives on mental well-being, he pioneered Cognitive Behavioral Therapy (CBT). His vision has since empowered therapists, educators, and individuals worldwide, emphasizing the transformative power of positive thought.

From Weeds to Blooms

Every garden, no matter how overrun by weeds, has the potential to bloom. All it needs is care, attention, and the right interventions. Nigel's journey from a troubled youth to a beacon of hope serves as a testament to this. Through understanding, therapy, and unwavering faith, even the most challenging landscapes can be transformed.

As we turn the page on this chapter, let's carry forward a singular message: With the right care, every individual, every 'weed,' has the potential to bloom brilliantly in the garden of life.

L♥E
CBT

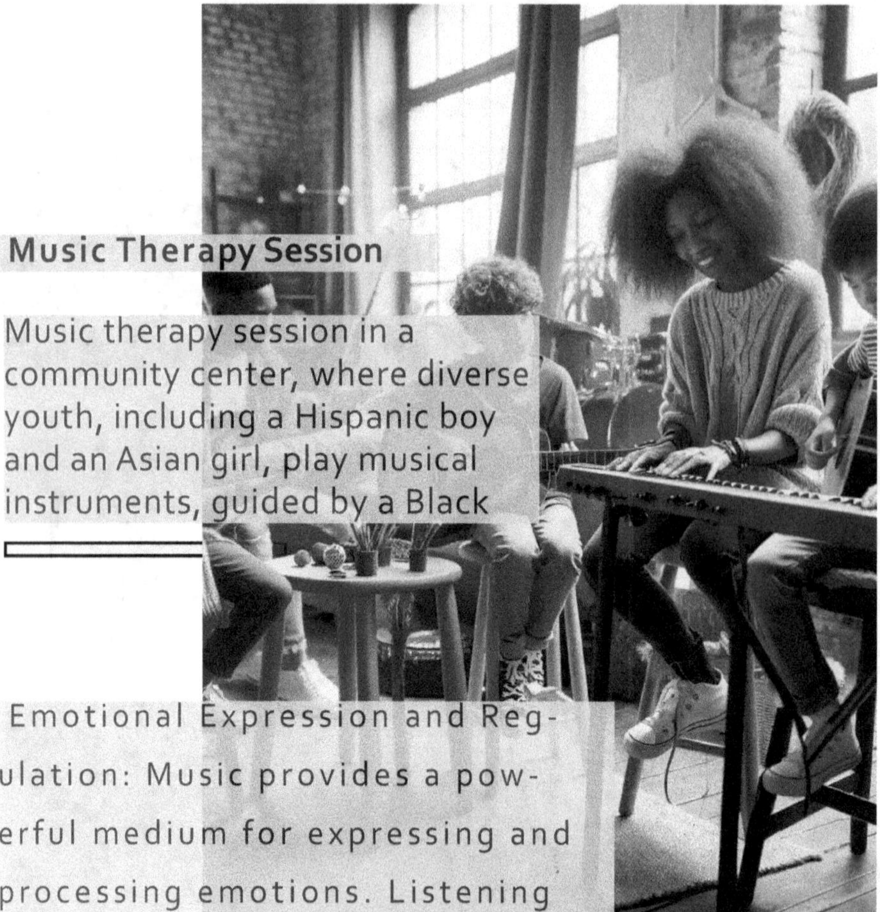

Music Therapy Session

Music therapy session in a community center, where diverse youth, including a Hispanic boy and an Asian girl, play musical instruments, guided by a Black

Emotional Expression and Regulation: Music provides a powerful medium for expressing and processing emotions. Listening to music can evoke a wide range of emotions, helping people to understand and articulate their feelings. Creating music, whether through singing, playing an instrument, or composing, offers an outlet for emotional expression and can be particularly therapeutic.

Cognitive Benefits: Music engages several areas of the brain,

Environmental Project in Urban Park

An image showing a young Asian girl and a Middle-Eastern boy participating in a community-led environmental project, planting trees in an urban park, demonstrating commitment to environmental stewardship.

Community Engagement and Responsibility: Participating in park cleanups helps youth understand the importance of taking care of their environment. It instills a sense of community responsibility and pride, showing them that their actions can make a tangible difference in their neighborhoods.

Chapter 3

Watering Seeds of Positivity

The morning sun cast a gentle glow on the community garden, a symbol of collective endeavor to foster growth amidst the concrete jungle of the city. Here, the Gardeners of the Mind convened, a group forged to delve into the therapeutic realms of Cognitive Behavioral Therapy (CBT).

As the members assembled, each carried with them stories of resilience and hope. Among them were parents, educators, and individuals who had faced the harsh realities of the juvenile justice system, a system that disproportionately ensnared the youth of color.

Their discourse often circled back to the representation of minority children in juvenile detention homes. The statistics were stark, sketching a narrative of systemic disparity that seemed to smother the potential right out of these young lives.

For every 100,000 Black youth, 152 found themselves confined within the cold bars of detention centers. Hispanic youth, though lesser in number, were not spared from the grasp of a system that seemed to have abandoned them long before they entered those ominous hallways.

The garden seemed to embody the antithesis of those cold, unforgiving places. Here, under the nurturing gaze of the sun, seeds of hope were being sown. The members meticulously tended to the garden, each plant a testament to their resolve to alter the narrative.

The group leader, a compassionate therapist, often drew parallels between the growth of plants and the nurturing of the mind. She reiterated that just like plants, the mind too yearned for tender care, sunlight, and the occasional pruning of negative thoughts.

As the garden flourished, so did the minds of the Gardeners. Through CBT, they unearthed the art of positive affirmations, a tool that held the power to alter the internal dialogues that often spiraled into abysses of despair.

They shared stories of their encounters with a system seemingly designed to keep them ensnared in a cycle

CBT
CBT
CBT Thrive 
Cognitive Behavioral Therapy City
BLACK
LIVES
MATTER

of negativity. The tale of St. Battels Clinic was one such narrative that resonated with many.

The lingering odor of sewer water still haunted the memories of those who had been there. The endless waiting in cold, unwelcoming lobbies seemed to stretch not just hours, but hope thin. The stark contrast of their experiences in well-resourced communities was a bitter truth to swallow.

But amidst the bitter reality, the sweet essence of hope lingered in the air as the Gardeners delved deeper into the principles of CBT. They learned to challenge and change the patterns of negative thinking that had become their unwanted companions over the years.

In the sanctuary of the garden, the bitter words of disparagement from past teachers and society were replaced by the nurturing affirmations of self-worth. Each seed they planted in the soil seemed to parallel a seed of positivity planted in the furrows of their minds.

They began to understand the profound impact of environment on growth, both of plants and minds. The stark difference between the nurturing ambiance of the garden and the oppressive atmosphere of the juvenile detention centers was a vivid testament to what could be achieved with the right kind of nurture.

The narrative of St. Battels Clinic emerged again as they dissected the hurdles faced in seeking mental health care. The haunting memory of long waits, the odor of despair, and the indifference encountered was a harsh reality they all had navigated at some point.

The discourse shifted to the glaring differences in mental health treatment access. The numbers were telling; while in well-resourced communities, mental health care was within arm's reach, in underserved areas, it was a distant dream.

They delved into the data, dissecting the glaring disparities. The group echoed the sentiment that one's skin color or zip code should not dictate the quality and accessibility of mental health care.

The tales of individuals waiting for hours in cold, uninviting lobbies while others in more affluent areas were swiftly attended to, resonated through the garden, striking a chord of collective resolve to challenge the status quo.

They saw themselves as the gardeners of change, each positive affirmation a watering can nurturing the seeds of systemic change. The garden became a microcosm of the world they envisioned, a place where growth was nurtured, and weeds of negativity were meticulously uprooted.

The ripple effect of their collective endeavor was palpable. The once wilted flowers of self-esteem slowly began to stand tall, basking in the newfound sunlight of self-compassion and understanding.

As they tended to the garden, they shared tales of how CBT had played a monumental role in altering their internal landscapes. The once barren grounds of hope were now fertile with positive affirmations, changing the narrative one thought at a time.

They began reaching out beyond their garden, sharing the seeds of knowledge and positivity with other communities, transcending the boundaries that had once kept them isolated in despair.

The cinematic tales of transformation reverberated through the community, inspiring many to take up the spade and hoe of self-reflection, to tend to the gardens of their minds.

The discussions in the garden transcended the personal realm, venturing into the systemic. They dissected the data, laying out the facts like a lawyer

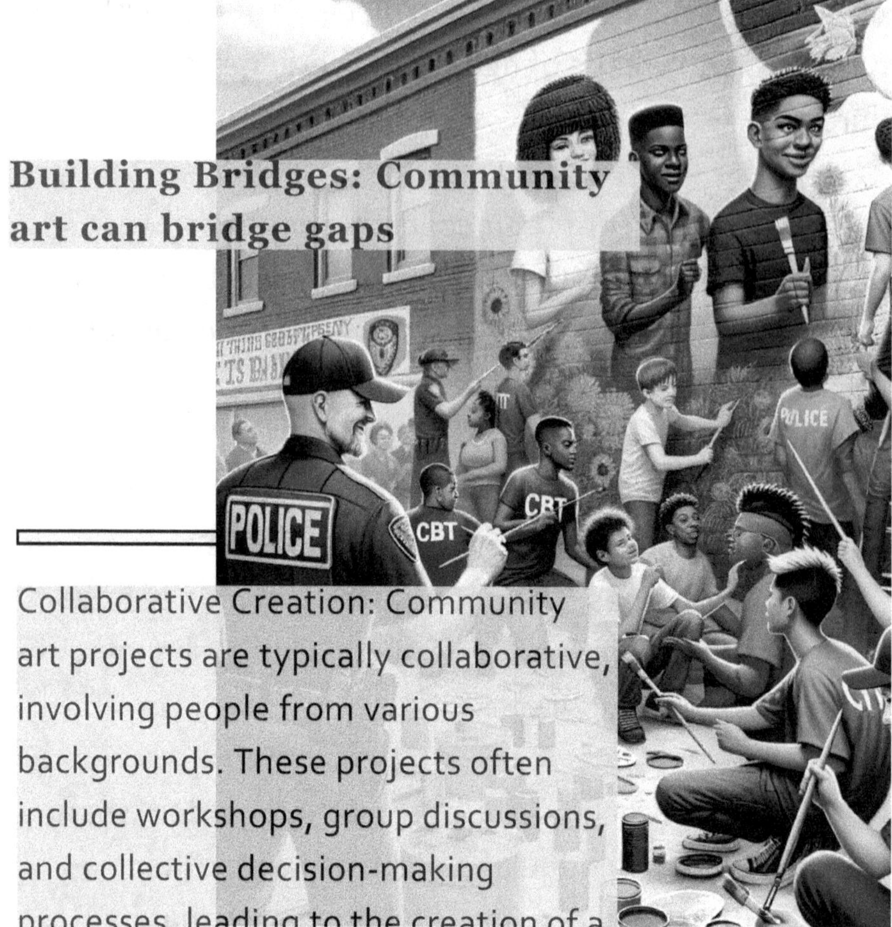

Building Bridges: Community art can bridge gaps

Collaborative Creation: Community art projects are typically collaborative, involving people from various backgrounds. These projects often include workshops, group discussions, and collective decision-making processes, leading to the creation of a shared piece of art.

Community Art Project: In-ner-city youth

Social Engagement: Community art is a powerful tool for social engagement. It brings people together, fostering a sense of community and belonging. Through art, individuals can share their experiences, learn from others, and build relationships.

presenting a compelling case to the jury.

The group began engaging with local authorities, presenting the glaring disparities in juvenile detention and mental health care access. Their stories, backed by irrefutable data, were their strongest evidence.

They were no longer just victims of the system but were emerging as the architects of change. The garden was a living testament to what could be achieved with the right blend of resolve, community support, and evidence-based therapeutic interventions like CBT.

The garden bore witness to their journey from being ensnared in the thorny vines of systemic oppression to becoming the gardeners of their minds, nurturing seeds of hope amidst a landscape that often seemed barren.

The tales from St. Battels Clinic and the juvenile detention centers were no longer just tales of despair but were transforming into narratives of hope and a clarion call for systemic change.

Each day as they gathered in the garden, the horizon seemed to be expanding. The oppressive walls of the past were replaced by open skies of possibilities. The garden was their canvas, and they were painting a narrative of change with hues of hope, resilience, and collective endeavor.

The once oppressive narrative of minority children entangled in the juvenile justice system began to witness a crack, allowing the rays of hope to seep in, promising a dawn of change.

The garden was not just a place of solace, but a hub of action, a platform where the narrative was being rewritten, one seed of positive affirmation at a time.

As they watered the plants, they were also watering the seeds of change within and beyond, ready to blossom into a garden of hope that promised to challenge and change the systemic weeds choking the growth of many a promising life.

Cultural Awareness and CBT in Therapy:

CBT can be adapted to be culturally sensitive. Therapists can use knowledge of a patient's cultural background to better understand their worldview, which can be essential in forming a therapeutic alliance and in the successful application of CBT techniques.

Community and Support Networks: Events like this illustrate the importance of community and support networks, which are often integral to the healing process in CBT. The sense of belonging and acceptance can be therapeutic and reinforce the social aspect of mental health.

CBT recognizes the importance of individual differences and the need for personalized treatment ap-

Chapter 4

Growth in Adversity - CBT for
Challenging Environments

In the heart of the city's labyrinth, amidst the concrete and shadowed alleys, gardens of young minds strive to flourish. These are the high-risk neighborhoods, often overlooked and underestimated, where resilience is not just a trait but a necessity for survival. Here, amidst the thorns of adversity – poverty, bullying, and mental health struggles – grow the souls of tomorrow. Yet, these gardens are not barren; they are ripe for nurturing through the transformative power of Cognitive Behavioral Therapy (CBT).

In these urban meadows, where public aid is the lifeline and mental health discussions are rare blooms, CBT emerges not just as a therapeutic method but as a beacon of hope. It's a tool for survival and growth, a way to cultivate resilience and positivity in a terrain often harsh and unforgiving. This is a world where self-talk can often be a thicket of negativity, where the potential for self-harm and despair runs rampant like unchecked weeds.

CBT in these environments is more than therapy; it's a lifeline, a ray of light guiding the way through the fog of challenges. Like a diligent gardener, CBT helps to prune the harmful thoughts, to water and nurture the seeds of positivity, and to provide the tools for these young minds to not just survive, but to thrive. It is here, in these communities, that CBT can don the cape of a superhero, offering a new narrative, a different perspective – a pathway to a life filled with hope and possibilities.

Our journey through this chapter is akin to walking through these gardens of young minds, understanding their struggles, and witnessing the miraculous growth that CBT can foster. We delve into the soil of their experiences, explore the roots of their challenges, and celebrate the blossoming of their resilience. Through the lens of CBT, we aim to transform these environments, one life at a time, proving that even in the most challenging terrains, there is always room for growth, for hope, and for a future where every individual feels valued, understood, and empowered.

Beneath the towering structures and bustling streets, in the heart of these high-risk areas, lies a tapestry of challenges, each thread weaving into the lives of its youngest inhabitants. Here, the air is thick not just with

Role-playing exercise to practice coping strategies for dealing with peer pressure and stress, with a CBT therapist facilitating the session.

Behavioral Activation: CBT often involves behavioral activation, which encourages individuals to engage in meaningful activities that align with their values and interests. Participating in cultural events can be an example of such activity, providing engagement, joy, and a sense of accomplishment.

Stress Reduction: Enjoyable community events can reduce stress and promote mental well-being, consistent with the goals of CBT to help individuals lead happier, more fulfilled lives.

pollution but with the echoes of strife – the sirens of emergency, the whispers of substance misuse, and the shadows of violence that loom like ominous clouds.

In these alleys and playgrounds, young minds are like saplings in a storm, often bending under the weight of adversity. The roots of their struggles run deep, nourished by the soil of poverty and the drought of opportunity. Their daily reality is a labyrinth of obstacles, where each turn could lead to danger or despair.

Yet, in this concrete jungle, there is a resilient beat, a pulse of life that refuses to be stifled. It is in these very streets, where the challenges are most daunting, that the potential for transformation is greatest. Here, Cognitive Behavioral Therapy steps in like a gardener armed with tools of hope and change. CBT doesn't just aim to trim the overgrown weeds of trauma and hardship; it seeks to replant, to instill new seeds of thought and behavior that can withstand the storms.

As we delve further into this chapter, we explore how CBT can be intricately woven into the fabric of these communities. Through schools and community centers, this therapeutic approach becomes accessible, a beacon of guidance and support. CBT offers a mirror for self-reflection and a map for navigating the complex maze of emotions and experiences.

Community members actively engaged in planting seeds in a garden within their neighborhood.

Individuals and families working together, tending to the soil in a communal garden space. The backdrop of the urban landscape symbolizes growth and renewal in the city's heart. The garden acts as a metaphor for nurturing and hope, with people of all ages contributing to the revitalization of their shared environment.

A garden is a lot like CBT (Cognitive Behavioral Therapy). Just like CBT helps us nurture our minds and grow in a positive way, a garden lets us cultivate and tend to the soil of our souls.

In both, we start with a seed of thought or a tiny plant, representing our current state. Through CBT, we plant the seeds of new perspectives, challenging negative thoughts, and nurturing positive ones. In the garden, we sow seeds and care for them, watching as they sprout and flourish.

In the hands of dedicated therapists and empathetic community workers, CBT transforms into an instrument of empowerment. It equips these young minds with the skills to reshape their narrative, to recognize the weeds of negative self-talk and to cultivate a garden of self-worth and resilience.

Together, in these pages, we journey through this transformative process, witnessing the growth of individuals and communities. We see how, one life at a time, the landscape of these high-risk areas can be altered – not by erasing the challenges, but by changing how they are faced and overcome.

In the dense thicket of city life, where shadows loom larger than dreams, we find Marcus. A formidable figure in the schoolyard, Marcus wears his bravado like armor, a shield against his own inner turmoil. To his peers, he's the quintessential bully, a storm of anger and aggression. But beneath this façade lies a tumultuous sea of depression and anxiety, invisible to the naked eye.

One brisk morning, as the schoolyard buzzes with the energy of a new day, Marcus corners Alex, a quiet, introspective boy with a love for books.

"Hey, nerd!" Marcus bellows, his voice echoing off the school walls, "What's with the book? Planning to fly away on a fantasy?"

Alex, trembling slightly but maintaining his composure, replies, "Books are my escape. They take me places where I feel... safe."

Marcus sneers, "Safe, huh? You need to toughen up, not hide in fairytales."

Their exchange is overheard by Ms. Thompson, a keen-eyed teacher with a gentle heart. She approaches calmly, sensing the pain that fuels Marcus's aggression.

Teenager sitting thoughtfully on a curb in an urban environment. Behind him is a large, detailed mural on a brick wall, vividly depicting a journey from darkness to light with symbolic imagery such as breaking chains, opening doors, and rising suns. This imagery represents overcoming challenges. The teenager, dressed in casual clothing, has an expression of deep reflection and newfound understanding, embodying a transformation influenced by CBT principles.

"Marcus," she says softly, "I see a lot of strength in you, but I also see a fight. Are you fighting dragons in your own story?"

Marcus, caught off guard by her insight, falters. "I... I don't know what you mean."

Ms. Thompson nods, understanding. "Sometimes, our biggest battles are within us. You're not alone in this. Let's talk."

This moment marks the beginning of a turning point. Through guided CBT sessions with Ms. Thompson, Marcus starts to unravel the knots of his depression and anxiety. He learns to understand his emotions, to express rather than suppress them. Gradually, the schoolyard bully begins to transform into a protector, using his strength to uplift rather than intimidate.

In tandem, Alex, the once-intimidated student, finds his voice too. He learns to assert himself, to stand tall amidst adversity, drawing strength from his own resilience and the understanding that even the fiercest storms have a calm center.

This story of transformation, a testament to the power of CBT, reflects the dual nature of struggle. It high-

Standing around a makeshift memorial to honor a young life that was tragically lost. The expressions of sorrow and mutual support are evident as they hold candles and stand in silent tribute.

'CBT Thrive' poster in an urban environment, possibly on a busy street or in a public space.

lights how pain, when acknowledged and addressed, can lead to growth and change, not just for the individual but for the community as a whole. It's a narrative of hope, showing that even in the toughest environments, change is possible, one life, one story at a time.

Continuing our exploration, we delve deeper into the dynamics of the school environment, a microcosm of the broader community. Here, we encounter Sarah, a bright student who excels academically but struggles socially. She often becomes the target of ridicule due to her shy nature and academic focus.

One day, during a particularly challenging group project, Sarah finds herself the subject of harsh words from her peers. "Why do you always have to be so perfect, Sarah? It makes the rest of us look bad," taunts one of her classmates.

Crushed by these words, Sarah retreats into her shell, her confidence wavering. This incident, however, catches the attention of Mr. Johnson, the school counselor, known for his empathetic approach and deep understanding of student dynamics.

Approaching Sarah with a gentle smile, Mr. Johnson invites her to share her thoughts. "Sarah, I've noticed you've been a bit withdrawn lately. Want to talk about what's going on?"

Hesitantly, Sarah opens up about her feelings of isolation and the pressures of being labeled as the 'smart one'. Mr. Johnson listens intently, validating her emotions and gently introducing the principles of CBT. Together, they work on strategies to cope with social anxiety and to reframe her thoughts about her academic success.

Through their sessions, Sarah begins to see her intelligence not as a barrier, but as a bridge connecting her to others. She learns to communicate her feelings more effectively and to find common ground with her peers. Her journey, while personal, has a ripple effect, influencing the classroom dynamics. Students start to recognize and appreciate the diversity in their strengths and weaknesses, fostering a more inclusive and supportive environment.

This transformation in Sarah and her classmates underscores the profound impact of CBT in reshaping not just individual perspectives but also collective attitudes. It demonstrates how empathy and understanding can turn challenges into opportunities for growth, building a community where everyone feels valued and connected.

Our story begins in a CBT session, where we meet our bully, Marcus. He's a tall, broad-shouldered teenager with a scowl that's become his shield. As he sits, arms crossed, in the therapist's office, his tough exterior begins to crack under the gentle probing of Dr. Andrews, a warm, middle-aged therapist with a knack for reaching troubled youths.

Dr. Andrews: "Marcus, let's talk about what happened at school yesterday."

Marcus, hesitant at first, eventually opens up about his actions and feelings. We hear the pain in his voice, the confusion and fear that drive his aggression.

Marcus: "I don't know, Doc. It's like... when I'm out there, it's all a blur. I feel powerful, but then... it's just emptiness."

The scene shifts to another CBT session with one of Marcus's victims, Sarah, a bright-eyed girl who's lost her spark. Sarah sits across from Ms. Garcia, a young, empathetic therapist.

Ms. Garcia: "Sarah, can you tell me how you felt when Marcus spoke to you that way?"

Sarah: "Scared... and small. Like I couldn't do anything right."

As the sessions progress, we see a transformation. Marcus begins to understand the root of his anger and learns healthier ways to express his emotions. He starts to grasp the impact of his actions.

Marcus: "I never realized how much I was hurting them... I was just trying to deal with my own stuff."

Meanwhile, Sarah learns coping strategies and starts regaining her confidence. She even finds the courage to confront her fears.

Sarah: "I know I can't control what others do, but I can control how I respond, how I let it affect me."

The climax of our story is a carefully orchestrated meeting between Marcus and his victims, supervised by their therapists. It's a tense, emotional encounter, filled with apologies, understanding, and a tentative step towards forgiveness.

Marcus: "I'm sorry for what I did. I was dealing with a lot, and I took it out on you. I'm learning to be better."
Sarah: "I accept your apology, Marcus. It's been hard, but I'm learning too. We all are."

The chapter concludes with a sense of closure and

hope. The playground, once a place of fear, starts to heal, reflecting the inner transformation of our characters. Marcus, no longer a bully, begins to make amends, and Sarah and the others find strength they never knew they had.

Chapter 5

The Right Tools - CBT Exercises

for Teens

In the heart of a bustling city, where the noise of life never ceases, there's a small elementary school, a beacon of hope and learning. Here, amidst the chatter of young minds, a new chapter begins in the lives of two remarkable children, Emma and Lucas, who are about to discover the transformative power of Cognitive Behavioral Therapy (CBT).

The Playground Discovery

Emma, a bright-eyed 8-year-old with a love for stories, encounters Lucas, a 10-year-old with a penchant for puzzles, on the school playground. Lucas is often overwhelmed by anxiety, while Emma struggles with bouts of sadness.

Emma: "Hey Lucas, why do you always look so worried?"

Lucas: "I can't help it, Emma. Sometimes, my thoughts just race like crazy."
As they talk, Ms. Harper, their compassionate teacher, approaches, overhearing their conversation. She smiles gently, sensing an opportunity to introduce them to the world of CBT.

Ms. Harper: "Lucas, Emma, have you ever heard of CBT? It's like a toolbox for your mind."
The Classroom Adventure
In the classroom, Ms. Harper turns CBT into an adventure. She lays out a colorful mat, resembling a board game, and hands Emma and Lucas playful tokens.

Ms. Harper: "This game will help us explore your thoughts and feelings. Each square is a challenge to understand and transform our thoughts."

As they play, Emma and Lucas start to open up, sharing their fears and worries, turning them into stories and puzzles.

Emma: "I sometimes feel like I'm in a sad story with no

happy ending."

Lucas: "And I feel like I'm trapped in a puzzle I can't solve."

Ms. Harper: "Let's rewrite that story, and find the solution to that puzzle, together."

The Family Involvement
One evening, Emma and Lucas bring the CBT game home. Their families gather around, curious and supportive. The living room transforms into a space of shared learning and healing.

Emma's Mom: "This game is not just for Emma, it's for us too. We're all part of her story."

Lucas' Dad: "And we can help solve the puzzle, one piece at a time."The Community Impact

Back at school, Emma and Lucas become ambassadors of CBT. They start a club, inviting other kids to play the game, share stories, and solve puzzles. The school community begins to buzz with a new energy of understanding and empathy.

Emma: "Look, Lucas! We're not just changing our sto-

'ALL Lives Matter' Black, Hispanic, White, Palestinians, Israeli, and Asian

A peaceful protest focusing on the 'All Lives Matter' movement. The scene shows a diverse group of protesters, including people of various descents such as Black, Hispanic, White, and Asian, holding signs and banners advocating for the value of all human lives. The setting is an urban environment, with the crowd gathered on a city street, surrounded by buildings. The protesters are depicted in a peaceful and respectful manner, emphasizing the message of universal human dignity and equality. The atmosphere conveys a sense of unity and commitment to inclusivity and mutual respect among all people.

ries; we're changing everyone's!"

Lucas: "We're puzzle solvers, Emma. We're finding the pieces that fit perfectly for each of us."

Expanding the Circle

With the success of their CBT club, Emma and Lucas decide to expand their reach. They partner with Ms. Harper to organize a school-wide workshop. The gymnasium is filled with colorful mats, each a station for different CBT activities.

Lucas: "We've got to make this fun and engaging for everyone!"

Emma: "Yes, and let's share our stories too. It's not just about playing; it's about connecting."

The workshop is a hit. Students from different grades participate, sharing their thoughts and learning new coping strategies. The atmosphere is vibrant, filled with laughter and earnest conversations.

The Ripple Effect

As news of their initiative spreads, a local psychologist, Dr. Jensen, visits the school. Impressed by their approach, she offers to conduct a special session for parents and teachers.

Dr. Jensen: "What you kids have started here is remarkable. You're not just learning CBT; you're living it and sharing it."

During the session, adults learn alongside the children, gaining insights into their world and understanding the value of CBT in everyday life.

Overcoming Challenges

Weeks pass, and the impact of the CBT club becomes evident. Students who once struggled with anxiety, like Lucas, or sadness, like Emma, are now more confident and expressive.

Emma: "I never thought I could feel so...light. It's like I've rewritten my story."

Lucas: "And I've solved a part of my puzzle. There are still pieces to place, but now I know I can do it."

The School Assembly

To celebrate their journey, the school hosts an assembly. Emma and Lucas take the stage, sharing their experiences and the lessons they've learned. The audience is captivated, moved by their honesty and bravery.

Lucas: "CBT isn't just a game or a set of tools. It's a way to understand ourselves and each other."

Emma: "And it's about hope. No matter how tough things get, there's always a way to make it better."

Looking Forward

As the chapter nears its end, we see Emma, Lucas, and their peers looking forward to a future where mental well-being is a shared journey. The school continues to nurture this environment, making CBT an integral part of its culture.

The graduate stands at a podium, addressing the audience with confidence and enthusiasm.

Chapter 6

The Crossroads of Youth - Choices
and Consequences

The sun beamed down on the sea of caps and gowns, creating a vibrant mosaic in the courtyard of the high school. It was a day of endings and beginnings - graduation day. James stood at the podium, his heart pounding in his chest as he looked out at his classmates, his football teammates, and the sea of faces that represented the journey they had all undertaken together.

"Friends, mentors, and fellow graduates," James began, his voice steady despite the turmoil within. "Today marks not just the end of our high school journey, but the beginning of our path into adulthood. We've tackled challenges on the field, aced (and sometimes barely passed) our exams, and forged friendships that will last a lifetime."

The crowd listened, hanging onto his words. James continued, "But the true test lies ahead. It's in the choices we make, the paths we choose, and how we decide to face the world outside these walls. Let's make those choices count. Let's be the best versions of ourselves."

As the ceremony concluded, James felt a sense of pride mixed with apprehension. The world outside the school gates was a stark contrast to the one he was leaving behind. The streets of his neighborhood whispered with the echoes of paths not taken, choices that led down darker roads.

Ronnie, once his closest friend, now symbolized the life James had been steering clear of. They had grown up like brothers, their lives intertwining like the streets of their neighborhood. But as time passed, their paths diverged - Ronnie into the world of gangs, and James clinging to the values his family had instilled in him.

One evening, as James returned from school, he saw Ronnie sitting in a sleek car, a stark contrast to the run-down buildings that lined their street. "Yo, James! Come here, man!" Ronnie called out, a playful grin on his face.

James approached hesitantly, his heart racing. Ronnie flashed a wad of cash, a symbol of the life he led - a life

James and Ronnie

Here is the photorealistic image depicting James and Ronnie, two African-American men in their 20s, having a conversation on an urban street corner. James, dressed in casual business attire, is standing and engaging in conversation with Ronnie, who is in casual streetwear and leaning against a sleek car.

The urban setting, complete with brick buildings, a sidewalk, and street signs, frames their interaction. The image captures the essence of their different life choices and the depth of their conversation, reflecting their longstanding friendship and the complexities of life in the city.

full of easy money and dangerous shortcuts. "Here, take this. Buy something nice," Ronnie said, handing James a few bills.

James accepted the money, a knot forming in his stomach. It was a small gesture, but it represented so much more - the allure of a life that seemed out of reach, the seductive call of the streets.

One fateful night, under the dim glow of streetlights, Ronnie and James found themselves in a deep conversation. They talked about their lives, their struggles, and the dreams that seemed so distant now. Ronnie's words were a mix of nostalgia and a harsh dose of reality.

"Man, we used to run these streets together," Ronnie said, his voice laced with a mix of sadness and resignation. "But look at us now. I'm out here, and you're... you're just stuck, man."

James felt the weight of his friend's words. He was at a crossroads, torn between the life he knew and the one that beckoned him with false promises.

Then, in a moment that would change everything, Ronnie offered James a blunt. "Come on, man. Just one hit. It won't change anything," he urged.

the photorealistic image that symbolizes the responsibility of society to recognize and nurture the potential
in every individual.

James hesitated, the conflict raging within him. But the bond they shared, the memories of a shared childhood, and the desire to belong, to not be the odd one out, overwhelmed him. He took the blunt, inhaling deeply, letting the smoke fill his lungs.

As the haze of marijuana enveloped him, James felt a sense of betrayal - to his family, his beliefs, and most importantly, to himself. It was a moment of surrender, a step down a path he had long resisted.

This chapter in James's life was a poignant reminder of the power of choices and the impact they have. It was a turning point, marking the beginning of a journey that would test his values, his resolve, and ultimately, his identity.

As he sat with Ronnie, his childhood friend turned gang member, on the hood of an old car, they shared memories of simpler times. Ronnie's voice, tinged with nostalgia, broke the silence. "Man, James, remember how we dreamed of a better life? Now look at us, deep in the same mess we wanted to escape." James, his eyes reflecting the city lights, nodded silently. He thought about their dreams, now overshadowed by the reality of their lives.

The conversation shifted to the gang – their new family. Ronnie's words were convincing. "We've got each other's backs here. This is where we belong." James felt a sense of belonging, a bond forged in the struggles and shared experiences of street life.

The streets, with their relentless pull, had become a permanent fixture in his life. Engulfed in the world of gangs, his days were a blur of weed, alcohol, and an unyielding sense of loyalty to his newfound brothers.

It was during this tumultuous period that James stumbled upon an old acquaintance, Marcus, in the most unexpected of places. Marcus, once notorious for his unruly ways in school, had undergone a remarkable transformation. They met on a street corner, the city's cacophony forming a backdrop to their conversation.

"Yo, James! Man, it's been a minute," Marcus greeted him with a familiar grin. His demeanor had changed; there was a newfound clarity in his eyes.

As they talked, Marcus shared his journey of redemption, attributing his turnaround to Cognitive Behavioral Therapy (CBT). "You know, CBT changed the game for me. It's all about catching those crazy thoughts before they catch you," Marcus explained, his urban lingo making the concept more relatable to James.

Intrigued, James listened intently. Marcus spoke of how he learned to challenge his destructive thought patterns and behaviors, replacing them with healthier, more constructive ones. "It's like reprogramming your mind, man. Instead of trippin' on the negative, you start focusing on what's real and positive," Marcus added with a knowing look.

Their conversation delved deeper, with Marcus sharing personal anecdotes of his transformation. He talked about recognizing his self-destructive inner dialogue and learning to counter it with rational, empowering thoughts.

This encounter with Marcus planted a seed of curiosity in James. The idea that he could reshape his thoughts and, in turn, his life, was a revelation. For the first time in a long while, James felt a flicker of hope, a possibility of escaping the cycle he found himself trapped in.

James's journey towards change was gradual and fraught with challenges. Implementing the strategies of CBT in his daily life, especially amidst the chaos of the streets, was a daunting task. Yet, inspired by Marcus's transformation, he persevered.

Each day became a step towards a different future, one not dictated by the gang or the street. James learned to recognize and challenge the negative thoughts that had long influenced his actions.

Active
Listening

Chapter 7

In a bustling community center, James found himself amidst a CBT workshop aimed at enhancing communication skills. The room buzzed with a mix of apprehension and curiosity. James, once hesitant, now leaned forward, intrigued by the facilitator's approach.

"Communication isn't just about talking; it's about understanding," the facilitator began, capturing the room's attention. "Today, we'll explore how CBT can enhance our ability to express ourselves and understand others."

The first exercise involved role-playing. Participants paired up, practicing active listening and empathetic responses. James, paired with an older gentleman, initially struggled. As they exchanged stories, James realized the power of truly hearing someone.

Next, the group delved into emotional articulation.

Participants were encouraged to describe their feelings with precision, moving beyond generic terms like 'good' or 'bad'. James found this challenging but enlightening, as it helped him understand the complexity of his emotions.

The facilitator then introduced the concept of 'I' statements, a way to express feelings without placing blame. "It's about owning your emotions," she explained. James and the others practiced, slowly grasping how to communicate assertively yet respectfully.

In the serene ambiance of the CBT group session, the participants sat in a circle, each eager yet apprehensive about sharing their innermost thoughts. The facilitator, a woman with a gentle voice and a reassuring smile, encouraged openness and respect. As the session progressed, it was James' turn to share.

James cleared his throat, his eyes scanning the room, landing on each attentive face. "You know," he began, his voice steady yet tinged with vulnerability, "I've always been the type to hold things in, keep my troubles to myself. But, sitting here, I'm realizing how much that's been eating at me."

He paused, collecting his thoughts. "There was this time, not too long ago, when things got really tough. My family was struggling, and I felt like I had to be the strong one, you know? I'd sit in my room, just staring at the ceiling, wondering if anyone really understood what I was going through."

The group listened intently, their expressions a mix of empathy and understanding. James continued, his words flowing more freely now. "It's like I was trapped in my own head, constantly telling myself I wasn't good enough, that I couldn't make a difference. It was a dark place to be."

The facilitator nodded encouragingly, prompting him to delve deeper. "How did you start to change that narrative, James?" she asked gently.

James smiled faintly, a look of newfound clarity in his eyes. "Well, that's where CBT came in. It taught me to challenge those negative thoughts, to see them for what they really are – just thoughts, not facts. And slowly, I began to realize that I do have worth, that my feelings matter."

As James concluded, the room filled with a sense of collective relief and understanding. His story resonated with many in the group, who now felt inspired to share their own journeys.

The facilitator emphasized the importance of non-verbal cues. Participants learned to read body language and facial expressions, understanding how much communication is unspoken.

James found the segment on conflict resolution particularly relevant. The group role-played various scenarios, learning to navigate disagreements with calm and clarity.

As the workshop progressed, James felt a growing sense of community. Sharing experiences with strangers wasn't easy, but it was surprisingly therapeutic.

The facilitator then focused on empathy. "Understanding others' perspectives can transform conflicts," she said. Through various exercises, James and his peers practiced stepping into others' shoes.

One poignant exercise involved sharing personal struggles. James listened intently as others revealed their challenges, feeling a deep sense of connection.

The group also explored assertive communication. James learned to state his needs without aggression or passivity, a skill he knew would be invaluable.

In a powerful moment, James shared his journey with the group. Speaking candidly about his past, he felt a weight lifting off his shoulders.

As the workshop concluded, the facilitator reminded everyone that communication is a lifelong skill. "Keep practicing," she urged.

James left feeling empowered. The tools he'd gained weren't just theories; they were practical steps towards a better understanding of himself and others.

Back at home, James reflected on the day. The exercises, though simple, had sparked significant insights.

He realized that effective communication was key to mending and strengthening relationships. The lessons from the workshop echoed in his mind, a roadmap for the future.

In the days that followed, James noticed a change in his interactions. Conversations were deeper, more meaningful. He felt heard and understood.

This newfound skill wasn't just about speaking; it was about connecting. James embraced this journey, grateful for the unexpected ways CBT had enriched his life.

As the chapter closed, it was clear: communication was more than words. It was the bridge between hearts and minds, a path to mutual understanding and respect.

CBT exercise involving role-playing

Additionally, the image shows the group working on emotional articulation, with individuals of different backgrounds expressing their feelings. The setting is designed to be comfortable and inclusive, highlighting the diversity and unity of the group in the learning process.

The participants, representing various ethnicities and ages, are engaging in role-playing activities, practicing active listening and empathetic responses.

Chapter 8

The sun had barely crested the horizon when Marcus, a young African-American man, quietly tiptoed out of his modest bedroom, careful not to wake his sleeping wife, April, a Caucasian American woman, or their infant child. The walls of their small apartment were thin, and even the faintest sound seemed to echo. He paused for a moment, looking at April's peaceful face, a stark contrast to the turmoil he knew simmered beneath her calm exterior.

April had been struggling. Since the birth of their child, her bright, lively eyes had grown increasingly shadowed with the weight of postpartum depression. Anxiety, an unwelcome companion she hadn't known she harbored, now gripped her days and nights. Marcus had his own battles. He'd been wrestling with mental health issues, but recently, he'd found solace in Cognitive Behavioral

Couple who graduated
from high school at 17
and are now raising a
child.

April had been struggling.
Since the birth of their child,
her bright, lively eyes had
grown increasingly shadowed
with the weight of postpartum
depression

Therapy (CBT). It had become his lifeline, a way to navigate the choppy waters of his mind. But in his relief, he had neglected to share this beacon with April.

Their young marriage, a tender union formed fresh out of high school, was now facing the harsh realities of adulthood. The joy of new parenthood was overshadowed by the strain of mental health issues and the added complexity of navigating their differing ethnic backgrounds. The cultural nuances, once a source of fascination and unity, now seemed to only widen the gap between them.

One evening, as their baby finally settled into a restful sleep, April and Marcus found themselves in the living room, a space that felt smaller with each passing day. The silence was heavy, filled with unspoken thoughts and emotions. April, her eyes tired but defiant, broke the quiet.

"Marcus, we need to talk. I can't keep going like this," she began, her voice trembling slightly.

Marcus looked at her, his expression a mix of concern and hope. He had been waiting for this moment, a chance to bridge the gap between them.

So, you think you're better now?
That you've got it've all fugrred out??

"I know things have been hard, especially for you, April. I've been… I've been trying this thing, CBT. It's been helping me, a lot actually," he said hesitantly.

April's expression hardened. "So, you think you're better now? That you've got it all figured out?" she asked, a hint of bitterness lacing her words.

"No, no, it's not like that. It's just… It's given me tools, ways to cope. I should have shared it with you, I know that now," Marcus replied, his voice filled with regret.

April sighed, her anger ebbing away, replaced by a weary curiosity. "Tell me about it then. What is this CBT?"

Marcus explained, his words careful and measured. He talked about the strategies he learned for improving focus and motivation, how CBT helped him understand and reframe his thoughts, and how it could potentially aid April in her battle with postpartum depression and anxiety.

As they talked, something shifted in the room. The walls seemed to expand, giving them space to breathe. April, who had been skeptical at first, began to see the possibilities. She imagined a life where her thoughts didn't control her, where she could be present and enjoy being a mother, a wife.

The conversation stretched into the night, the couple delving deeper into how CBT could be integrated into their lives. They discussed how these strategies could not only help them as individuals but also strengthen their relationship and their ability to co-parent.

As dawn approached, a new understanding dawned between them. Marcus, seeing April's softened expression, dared to hope. April, feeling a flicker of hope herself, allowed a small smile to cross her lips. They were on the same team, fighting the same battle.

Their journey was just beginning, but for the first time in a long while, they felt equipped to face it together. With CBT as their tool, they were ready to harvest the success of their academic and personal lives, united in their struggle and their love.

She is depicted in a moment of confrontation

Chapter 9

Janie, a young school teacher with a gentle demeanor and an intuitive heart, stood at the front of her classroom, her gaze sweeping over the sea of young faces before her. These children, barely into their teenage years, already bore the weight of the world on their slender shoulders. Janie had noticed the subtle signs: the way some of them shrank into their seats, eyes downcast, or how laughter had become a rarity in the corridors. It pained her to see them grappling with depression and anxiety at such a tender age.

Determined to make a difference, Janie embarked on a mission. She wanted to arm her students with the tools they needed to combat these invisible foes. CBT, or Cognitive Behavioral Therapy, was the weapon she chose - a way to equip them with self-esteem, social skills, and the resilience to face peer pressure and social anxiety.

One day, she decided to address these issues head-on. The classroom buzzed with the usual pre-lesson chatter when Janie cleared her throat, signaling for silence. The room hushed as all eyes turned to her.

"Today, I want to talk about something important," Janie began, her voice steady and clear. "I know some of you are struggling. You feel like you're alone in this, that no one understands. But I want you to know, you're not alone."

The students shifted in their seats, some exchanging glances, others staring intently at Janie.

"Life can be overwhelming, especially at your age. Peer pressure, expectations, the fear of not fitting in... It can all lead to feelings of anxiety and depression. But there's a way to fight back."

Janie paced slowly in front of the classroom, her words resonating in the silent room.

"Cognitive Behavioral Therapy is a tool we can all use. It's about understanding our thoughts and emotions and learning how to control them, not letting them control us."

With CBT, we weed out destructive

With CBT, we weed out destructive thought patterns, just as we weed our garden beds to make room for the plants to thrive. And just as CBT encourages us to replace harmful thoughts with healthier ones, a garden blooms with vibrant flowers and fruitful crops, replacing weeds with beauty and sustenance.

Patience and Persistence: In both CBT and gardening, patience is key. Just as it takes time for new thought patterns to take root in CBT, it takes time for seeds to sprout and plants to mature in a garden. We must persistently nurture and care for them.

Rooting Out Negativity: Just as CBT encourages us to identify and uproot negative thought patterns, gardening requires us to identify and remove invasive weeds that can hinder the growth of our plants. This parallels the process of eliminating harmful influences from our lives.

Nurturing Growth:

Nurturing Growth: CBT teaches us to nurture healthier thought patterns, much like we water and provide nutrients to our plants. We offer support, encouragement, and self-compassion to ourselves, fostering positive growth.

Adapting to Change: In a garden, we must adapt to changing seasons and weather conditions. Similarly, CBT equips us with tools to adapt to life's challenges, helping us manage stress, anxiety, and setbacks more effectively.

and a sense of accomplishment.

Harvesting the Fruits of Labor: Ultimately, both CBT and gardening reward us for our efforts. In CBT, we reap the benefits of improved mental health and well-being, while in a garden, we enjoy the literal fruits of our labor — fresh produce, vibrant flowers,

A hand timidly rose from the back of the class. It belonged to Emma, a quiet girl who rarely spoke up.

"But Miss, how can we control our thoughts? They just... happen," Emma's voice was a mere whisper, but it echoed loud in the hushed room.

Janie smiled gently at her. "That's a great question, Emma. CBT teaches us to recognize negative thoughts and challenge them. It's like being a detective, examining evidence and finding the truth behind our feelings."

The class listened, captivated. Janie's passion was infectious, her belief in their ability to overcome their struggles palpable.

"To anyone here who's felt like giving up, who's felt unseen or unheard, I want you to know this: You matter. Your feelings are valid. And with the right tools, you can overcome anything. Let's learn these skills together, let's support each other."

As Janie spoke, a transformation began. Eyes that were once dull sparkled with curiosity. Slumped shoulders straightened. A sense of unity filled the room.

Over the following weeks, Janie incorporated CBT techniques into her lessons. She conducted role-plays, group discussions, and individual exercises, each designed to build self-worth and social competence. The students learned to identify negative thought patterns, to challenge them, and to replace them with positive affirmations.

The change in the classroom was tangible. Laughter returned, conversations grew, and students who once shied away from participation now raised their hands eagerly. They were learning not just academic subjects, but lessons in life; lessons in how to bloom with confidence, combat social anxiety, and engage with the world around them.

Janie watched her students grow, a proud smile on her face. She had ignited a spark, and now she watched it burn brightly, a beacon of hope in each young life she had touched.

Here is the image of a classroom scene where Emma, a quiet student, is asking a question.

CHAPTER 10

Resilience Through Seasons - CBT
for Life's Transitions

In a small, tightly-knit community where church stee-
ples dotted the skyline and hymns resonated through
the streets, the concept of mental health was often
intertwined with spiritual well-being. Here, families like
those of Sarah and Michael held firm to their faith, seeing it as a bastion against life's tumultuous waves. Yet,
as their children grew, navigating the treacherous waters of puberty and school transitions, the limitations of
addressing mental health solely through a spiritual lens
became evident.

Sarah, a devout churchgoer, believed in the power of
prayer and faith to heal all wounds. However, she began to notice changes in her son, Jacob, as he entered
his teenage years. His once bubbly demeanor had given
way to silence and isolation. Conversations about puberty, mental health, or emotional struggles were taboo

Here is the image of a Black woman from the city holding a 'CBT Thrive' poster in front of random people. The setting is an urban environment, possibly a street or public space, where she is presenting the poster to promote awareness about Cognitive Behavioral Therapy. The image captures the woman's enthusiasm and commitment to the cause, with a diverse group of people in their household, dismissed as issues that faith alone could resolve.

In stark contrast, Michael, a local pastor, openly embraced the concept of Cognitive Behavioral Therapy (CBT) alongside his deep-rooted faith. He saw the value in addressing the mental and emotional needs of his congregation, especially the youth, who were often caught between the expectations of their religious upbringing and the realities of modern life.

Michael organized a series of workshops in the community center, focusing on CBT techniques to help young people navigate life's transitions. He emphasized that while faith was crucial for spiritual guidance, CBT provided practical tools for managing thoughts, emotions, and behaviors in the natural world.

The sessions drew in teenagers and parents alike, curious and somewhat skeptical. Michael began by addressing the elephant in the room: the misconception that seeking mental health support indicated a lack of faith.

"CBT isn't about replacing our faith, but complementing it," Michael explained. "Our spiritual well-being is vital, but so is our mental health. They are two sides of the same coin."

He shared stories of individuals who, like Jacob, struggled silently, their mental health issues misconstrued as spiritual failings. Through CBT, they learned to articulate their feelings, challenge negative thought patterns, and develop coping strategies for life's challenges, all while maintaining their spiritual beliefs.

The workshops covered topics like dealing with peer pressure, managing the stress of school transitions, and understanding the physical and emotional changes of puberty. Interactive sessions, role-plays, and group discussions created a safe space for the youth to express themselves, a stark contrast to their usual reticence on such matters.

Sarah attended one of these workshops, initially out of curiosity, but soon found herself deeply engaged. The realization that her son's struggles were not a reflection of

his faith, but a natural part of growing up, was a revelation. She began to implement CBT techniques at home, encouraging open conversations and validating Jacob's feelings.

As the weeks passed, a transformation occurred within the community. Parents and children alike began to view mental health through a new lens, one that allowed for a balance between spiritual and psychological well-being. The stigma surrounding mental health discussions in religious households started to dissipate.

CBT provided the tools for resilience through life's transitions, complementing the community's spiritual foundation. It taught them that mental health care was not a sign of weakness, but a step towards holistic well-being. As Michael often said, "Our faith gives us hope, and CBT gives us the means to navigate the journey."

In this community, where once mental health was a whispered topic, conversations now flowed freely. The church remained a sanctuary for spiritual healing, but it also became a place where mental health was recognized as a crucial aspect of one's overall well-being. The integration of CBT into their lives didn't diminish their

faith; instead, it strengthened it, providing a compre-
hensive approach to resilience through life's ever-chang-
ing seasons.

The End